Also by Frederick Seidel

NICE WEATHER

NICE WEATHER

Frederick Seidel

FARRAR, STRAUS AND GIROUX
NEW YORK

Farrar, Straus and Giroux
18 West 18th Street, New York 10011

Library of Congress Cataloging-in-Publication Data
Seidel, Frederick, 1936–
    Nice weather / Frederick Seidel. — 1st ed.
    p.   cm.

    I. Title.

PS3569.E5 N53 2012
811'.54—dc23

                                    2011049909
    ISBN 9780374534059

Designed by Peter A. Andersen

www.fsgbooks.com

P1

TO KARL MILLER

CONTENTS

NICE WEATHER

NIGHT

The city sleeps with the lights on.
The insomniac wants it to be morning.
The quadruple amputee asks the night nurse what time it is.
The woman is asking for her mother,
But the mother is exhausted and asleep and long since dead.
The nun screams to stop the charging rhino
And sits bolt upright in bed
Attached to a catheter.

If a mole were afraid of the dark
Underground, its home, afraid of the dark,
And climbed out into the light of day, utterly blind,
Destroying the lawn, it would probably be caught and shot,
But not in the recovery room after a craniotomy.
The prostitute suspects what her client might want her to do.
Something is going on. Something is wrong.
Meanwhile, the customer is frightened, too.

The city sleeps with the lights on.
The garbage trucks come in the night and make noise and are gone.
Two angelfish swim around the room and out the window.
Laundry suns on a line beneath white summer cumulus.
Summer thunder bumbles in the distance.
The prostitute—whose name is Dawn—
Takes the man in her mouth and spits out blood,
Rosy-fingered Dawn.

STORE WINDOWS

I smile in the mirror at my teeth—
Which are their usual brown.
My smile is wearing a wreath.
I walk wreathed in brown around town.
I smile and rarely frown.

I find perfection in
The passing store windows
I glance at my reflection in.
It's citywide narcissism. Citizens steal a little peek, and what it shows
Is that every ugly lightbulb in that one moment glows.

A preposterous example: I'm getting an ultrasound
Of my carotid artery,
And the woman doing it, a tough transplanted Israeli, bends around
And says huskily, "Don't tell anybody
I said that your carotid is extraordinary."

I'm so proud!
It's so ridiculous I have to laugh.
The technician is very well endowed.
I'm a collapsible top hat—a *chapeau claque*—that half
The time struts around at Ascot but can be collapsed flat just like that. *Ba*

Till it pops back. *Paff!* Oh yes,
I find myself superb
When I undress.
A lovely lightbulb is my suburb,
And my flower, and my verb.

The naked man, after climbing the steps out of the subway,
Has moderate dyspnea, and is seventy-four.
He was walking down the street in Milan one day.
This was long ago. He began to snore.
He saw a sleeping man reflected in the window of a store.

THE YELLOW CAB

Tree-lined side streets make me lonely.
Many-windowed town houses make me sad.
The nicest possible spring day, like today, only
Ignites my inner suicide-bomber jihad.

I'm high on the fumes of my smokin' sunglasses,
But my exhaust pipe has a leak, which smells bad.
Take away my hack license. Open the windows. I'm passing gases.
A driver of a medallion taxi has gone completely mad.

Yellow cab, yellow cab, where have you been?
I've been to the mirror to try to look in.
Yellow cab, yellow cab, what found you there?
Soft contact lenses on four wheels and a fare.

The million leaves on the Central Park trees are popping
Open the champagne.
There's too much joy. There's no stopping.
Love is on top, fucking pain.

DOWNTOWN

July 4th fireworks exhale over the Hudson sadly.
It is beautiful that they have to disappear.
It's like the time you said I love you madly.
That was an hour ago. It's been a fervent year.
I don't really love fireworks, not really, the flavorful floating shroud
In the nighttime sky above the river and the crowd.
This time, because of the distance upriver perhaps, they're not loud,
Even the colors aren't, the patterns getting pregnant and popping.
They get bigger and louder when they start stopping.
They try to rally
At the finale.
It's the four-hundredth anniversary of Henry Hudson's discovery—
Which is why the fireworks happen on this side of the island this year.
Shad are back, and we celebrate the Hudson's Clean Water Act recovery.
What a joy to eat the unborn. We're monsters, I fear. What monsters we're.
We'll binge on shad roe next spring in the delicious few minutes it's here.

BEFORE AIR-CONDITIONING

The sweetness of the freshness of the breeze!
The wind is wiggling the trees.
The sky is black. The trees deep green.
The man mowing the enormous lawn before it rains makes goodness cle
It's the smell of laundry on the line
And the smell of the sea, brisk iodine,
Nine hundred miles inland from the ocean, it's that smell.
It makes someone little who has a fever feel almost well.
It's exactly what a sick person needs to eat.
Maybe it's coming from Illinois in the heat.
Watch out for the crows, though.
With them around, caw, caw, it's going to snow.
I think I'm still asleep. I hope I said my prayers before I died.
I hear the milkman setting the clinking bottles down outside.

MIDTERM ELECTION RESULTS, 2010

My old buddy, my body!
What happened to drive us apart?
Think of our trips to Bologna.
Think of our Ducati racebikes screaming.
We drank hypersonic grappa.

We got near the screaming Goyas.
What's blinding is Velázquez.
We never left the Prado—
And never saw Madrid!
That's what we did.

We met for lunch at the Paris Ritz.
We walked arm in arm
Through Place Vendôme.
Each put out a wrist
To try on a watch at Patek Philippe.

Unseparated Siamese twins,
We had to have the same girlfriend
And slept with her together.
We hopped on the Concorde,
Front cabin, seat 1.

Oh not to be meek and ache
And drop dead straining on the toilet seat.
Everyone on the sidewalk walks faster—
And didn't you use to walk
Springing up on the balls of your feet!

A single-engine light airplane
Snores in the slow blue dreamy afternoon.
This is our breakup.
We are down here falling apart.
The ocean crashes and crashes.

I put my arms around you—
But it's no good.
I climb the stairs—
It's not the same.
It's a flameout and windmill restart!

MIDWINTER

Midwinter murder is in my heart
As I stand there on the curb in my opera pumps,
Waiting for the car to come and the opera to start,
Amid the Broadway homeless frozen clumps.

Patent leather makes my shoes
Easter eggs by Fabergé.
The shoes say New York is still run by the Jews,
Who glitter when they walk, and aren't going away.

The morning after the Mozart, when I take my morning stroll, I feel
Removed all over again from the freezing suffering I see.
Someone has designed a beautiful, fully automatic, stainless steel,
Recoilless assault shotgun down in Tennessee.

The dogs tied up outside the Broadway stores
In the cold look with such touching expectancy inside.
A dog needs to adore. A dog adores.
A dog waiting for an owner is hot with identity and pride.

I'd like to meet the genius in Tennessee, or at least speak
To the gun on the phone.
I'd like to be both the dog owner and the dog. I'd leak
Love after I'd shot myself to shit. I'd write myself a bone.

SNOW

Snow is what it does.
It falls and it stays and it goes.
It melts and it is here somewhere.
We all will get there.

CHARLIE

IN MEMORY OF CHARLES P. SIFTON (1935–2009)

I remember the judge in a particular
Light brown chalk-stripe suit
In which he looked like a boy,
Half hayseed, half long face, half wild horse on the plains,
Half the poet Boris Pasternak with a banjo pick,
Plucking a twanging banjo and singing Pete Seeger labor songs.

I remember a particular color of
American hair,
A kind of American original orange,
Except it was rather red, the dark colors of fire,
In a Tom Sawyer hairstyle,
Which I guess means naturally

Unjudicial and in a boyish
Will Rogers waterfall
Over the forehead,
And then we both got bald . . .
My Harvard roommate, part of my heart,
The Honorable Charles Proctor Sifton of the Eastern District.

Charlie,
Harvard sweet-talked you and me into living in Claverly
Sophomore year, where no one wanted to be.
We were the elect, stars in our class selected
To try to make this palace for losers respected.
The privileged would light the working fireplaces of the rejected.

Everyone called you Tony except me, and finally—
After years—you told me you had put up with years of "Charlie"
From me, but it had been hard!
Yes, but when now
I made an effort to call you Tony, it sounded so odd to you,
You begged me to come back home. Your Honor,

The women firefighters you ruled in favor of lift their hoses high,
Lift their hoses high,
Like elephants raising their trunks trumpeting.
Flame will never be the same. Sifton, row the boat ashore.
Then you'll hear the trumpet blow.
Hallelujah!

Then you'll hear the trumpet sound.
Trumpet sound
The world around.
Flame will never be the same!
Sifton, row the boat ashore.
Tony and Charlie is walking through that door.

ARNOLD TOYNBEE, MAC BUNDY,
HERCULES BELLVILLE

Seventy-two hours literally without sleep.
Don't ask.
I found myself standing at the back
Of Sanders Theatre
For a lecture by Arnold Toynbee.

Standing room only.
Oxford had just published
With great fanfare Volume X of his interminable
Magnum opus, *A Study of History*.
McGeorge Bundy, the dean of the faculty,

Later JFK's
National Security Adviser, then LBJ's, came out onstage
To invite all those standing in the back
To come up onstage and use
The dozen rows of folding chairs already

Set out for the Harvard Choral Society
Performance the next day.
Bundy was the extreme of Brahmin excellence.
I floated up there in a trance.
His penis was a frosted cocktail shaker pouring out a cocktail,

But out came jellied napalm.
The best and the brightest
Drank the fairy tale.
The Groton School and Skull and Bones plucked his lyre.
Hercules Bellville died today.

He apparently said to friends:
"Tut, tut, no long faces now."
He got married on his deathbed,
Having set one condition for the little ceremony: no hats.
I knew I would lapse

Into a coma in full view of the Harvard audience.
I would struggle to stay awake
And start to fall asleep.
I would jerk awake in my chair
And almost fall on the floor. I put Hercky

In a poem of mine called "Fucking" thirty-one years ago, only
I called him Pericles in my poem.
At the end of "Fucking," as he had in life,
Hercules pulled out a sterling-silver-plated revolver
At a dinner party in London,

And pointed it at people, who smiled.
I had fallen in love at first sight
With a woman there I was about to meet.
One didn't know if the thing could be fired.
That was the poem.

NICE WEATHER

This is what it's like at the end of the day.
But soon the day will go away.
Sunlight preoccupies the cross street.
It and night soon will meet.
Meanwhile, there is Central Park.
Now the park is getting dark.

LONDON

The woman who's dying is trying to lose her life.
It's a great adventure
For everyone trying to help her.
Actually, death avoids her, doesn't want to hurt her.

So to speak, opens her hand and gently takes away the knife
Everyone well-meaning wants her to use on herself.
There is no knife, of course.
And she's too weak.

If you're too ill, the clinic near Zurich that helps
People leave this world won't.
If you're that medicated and out of it and desperate,
You may not be thinking right about wanting to end your life.

If you're near death, you may be *too* near
For the clinic to help you over the barrier.
She weakly screams she wants to die.
Hard to believe her pain is beyond the reach of drugs.

Please die. Please do. Her daughters don't want her to die and do.
The world of dew is a world of dew and yet
What airline will fly someone this sick?
They can afford a hospital plane but

Can she still swallow? The famous barbiturate cocktail
The clinic is licensed to administer isn't the Fountain of Youth.
But what if she gets there and drinks it and it only makes her ill?
And she vomits? It's unreal.

DINNER WITH HOLLY ANDERSEN

My fourteen books of poems
Tie a tin can to my tail.
You hear me fleeing myself.
I won't get away.
I went to Washington, D.C.

My agent hired a plane to tow the tail
Through the restricted airspace
Above the White House.
The tin can makes a noise,
As if I were in chains.

RUNAWAY SLAVE

VIOLATES AIRSPACE OVER NATIONAL AIR AND SPACE MUSEUM!
Fighter jets
From Andrews Air Force Base scramble
To intercept my fourteen books

And enter the East Wing
Of the National Gallery and the astonishment
Of the Vuillards,
Banking hard to lock in on the happy
Honking getaway convertible

Dragging sparks and tin cans as it musically pulls away,
The wedding guests having roared
Out of the reception and into the courtyard
To wave goodbye
With their champagne flutes to the joy.

BAUDELAIRE

I walk on water in my poems, using the lily pads
Of the sidewalk homeless as stepping-stones.
I'd stop to talk, but they don't have cell phones.
Their alcoholic faces come in various plaids.

A terrorist in his underwear,
Shaving in the steam, wipes the bathroom mirror clearer.
I see, while death is near, life is nearer.
My shaven skin is softer than the air.

The tugboat thrusts itself into the fluid to begin,
Backs out, chug, chug, tug, tug, digs in,
Que c'est bon, this is how, fowl and fang and fin.
The gulls, looking down at the meal down there, scream and grin.

His hands are in the basin washing, crashing.
His brain is on a boardwalk walking.
Her bigs don't stop stalking.
The mirror is asking for a thrashing.

I'm standing at a sideboard carving a wild duck I shot a lot.
My bullfrog croaks.
My unit smokes.
My Mumbai is hot. My Bali spits snot. I've shot what I've got.

Now it's time for the plane I'm on to come down
In pieces of women and men.
The anxiety increases in Yemen when
They pat me down in case I have something under my Muslim gown,

And I do.
I have a device.
In Paris, it had lice.
I went to Dr. Dax, who was distinguished. He knew.

Dax regarded my twenty-four-year-old thing
With barely disguised disgust.
I could see him thinking: I'm a doctor. It's his thing. I must.
O thing, where is thy sting? Dr. Dax made the prisoner sing.

It took a shirt of Nessus wrapped around my penis
To get rid of the crabs.
The burning ointment got lovingly applied by Babs—
Penis burned at the stake by Venus!

Babs of the beautiful *fesses*
Was Babette, comtesse d'Eeks.
Our Lady of the Heavenly Cheeks
Would turn over onto her stomach to receive a special caress.

In those days before airport security,
A terrorist could spread his wings and fly.
One poet lived his life in the sky,
While the maid did his laundry and a countess oiled his impurity.

The maid was Charles Baudelaire.
I live my life in the air.
Life is inherently unfair.
I don't care.

iPHOTO

The second woman shines my shoes.
The other takes my order, curtseys. Thank you, sir.
Others stand there in the rain so I can mount them when I choose.
It's how protective I
Can be that keeps them going. Look at her:
She clicks her heels together, bowing slightly. Try
To put yourself in her shoes: boots, garter belt, and veil.
She's amused
To be a piece of tail.
She's smiling. Is she really so amused? I've recused
Myself from judging whether that means she's abused.
So far I've refused
To let myself be called confused.
I hope these photos of St. Louis will be used.

A FRIEND OF MINE

"I walked in the door and into so much light
My eyesight did a kind of tremolo.
The living room began to snow
Cartwheels and pixels. You know what,

People's lives together are complicated.
They are quiet,
Complicatedly. My heart
And me get lost in the forest, afraid.

Yet I would choose you to lead me
To the clearing. I see
Your instincts are correct.
You ask the right questions.

You don't mind the answers!
When I move East for good next month
Maybe I will spread my wings
With happiness and soar.

Or I will shout *wheee* as I plummet downward.
Ah, but in my new New York apartment,
I am only on the fourth floor.
So I will hit the ground quickly!"

DO NOT RESUSCITATE

The mummy in the case is coming back to life.
It sits up slowly. I can't bear it.
The guard pays no attention. He knows it is my wife.
Her heart sits blinking on her shoulder like a parrot.

I get up from my bed, woozily embalmed, and it's
Another gorgeous New York day to try to live.
I loved my wife to bits in fits. I loved her tits.
Her bandaged mummy mouth had nothing else to give.

The man can't stay awake. He wakes and sleeps.
It's either age or it's his medications.
He's giving me the creeps—
All the poems he wrote, and so few dedications.

CIMETIÈRE DU MONTPARNASSE, 12ÈME DIVISION

I have a friend who has a friend
Who asked her to place her hand
And place a flower on Samuel Beckett's grave
On his behalf.
This man, who is in the theater, had corresponded with Sam.
My friend asked me to join her to do this.
It seemed reason enough to come to Paris.
And it was.
And there, quite a surprise, was Susan Sontag's grave.
And now it's time to get the fuck out
Of this beautiful pointlessness.

ROME

I impersonate myself and here I am,
Prick pointing at the moon, teeth sunk into your calf.
I ought to warn the concrete that my passion dooms the dam.
The poem I'm writing looks up at me and starts to laugh.

Summer! Of course you are! You are my miracle!
Just now we were in Rome.
I have to be in Rome with you to be so lyrical—
Or else it's noon Alaska time, the Auschwitz hour in Nome.

At Rockefeller Center, winter in New York, I pause.
Let's watch the skaters lark around the rink.
The worn-out dance floor of ice looks like a blind eye of gauze.
It's time to have a rinkside drink and have a little think.

I thought I'd never reach hydroplaning speeds again.
It's Sagaponack and the freezing April Atlantic.
Three, four, five, six, seven, eight, nine, ten . . .
It's about to happen. It's a feeling not dissimilar to being frantic.

Oh what a feeling. It's like America—
It's like Italy—with nothing else to compare it to.
Excitement mounts till *la repubblica italiana* is *isterica*!
Orgasm is an Italian opera aria of bombast and dew.

As in-your-face as a red Turkish fez
With a tassel—as hidden as an Israeli agent's gun—
"I'll call you back in five minutes," my vivid Italian girlfriend says
In English. Does she mean *cinque minuti italiani* or American?

In Via Michelangelo Caetani, near the Ghetto, where
The Red Brigades left Aldo Moro's body in the trunk of a parked car,
There's a plaque. There are flowers. I bow my head. I stare.
We've covered him with a blanket and I've shot him ten times so far.

A HISTORY OF MODERN ITALY

I see Silvio in a yellow slicker
Jumping up and down in a downpour,
Sing-songing *Rain rain go away,*
Come again another day.
His fists are clenched.
His nanny in a nurse outfit is smilingly drenched.
Silvio Berlusconi is not happy.
He feels crappy.

I'm talking to myself again.
I scroll down Broadway in the rain.
I'm hidden under an umbrella, but I hope it's obvious
I rejoice for Italy, more or less.
Not exactly talking to myself, more like quiet shouting.
I'm under a black umbrella spouting
A fancy accent (but I hate being taken for English). Yo!
Ooga-Booga says to Bunga Bunga: So long, Silvio!

We've circled to use up fuel
And now we're short final.
There's the rainy runway.
President Napolitano of Italy holds out his hand as if to say
Immortal blue from which no rain can fall
Fell. How to recover from a stall? Fall!
Brace for death. For landing.
Don't call it death. It's a matter of rebranding.

Cassius Clay turning into Muhammad Ali
Is the model of modernity.
Silvio Berlusconi is the *beau idéal* of hilarious iniquity.
The eurozone trees have rebranded into autumn. Italy is free!
Or rather Italy is sort of free.
The catastrophic lyrical elation of Leopardi
Described his country pityingly.
Then came Mussolini.

Duce! Duce! Duce! Adriano Visconti flew into the blue
In his heroic Macchi C.202
Like a pearl diver free-diving for pearls,
Or Berlusconi diving to the bottom for girls.
Fascist Visconti with his RAF mustache—
Such dash, such panache!
It was good to be an ace in World War II,
And rather better than being a Jew.

Visconti surrendered to communist partisans at Malpensa airfield—
Once they'd assured him no air or ground personnel of his would be killed
His personal safety was guaranteed by the mayor of Milan.
The Aeronautica Nazionale Repubblicana was done. Absolutely futile to
    fight on.
Visconti was respected.
The partisan commander saluted.
Visconti turned to walk across the courtyard to the espresso
The commander had offered, and was shot dead. Caro mio, addio.

MOUNT STREET GARDENS

I'm talking about Mount Street.
Jackhammers give it the staggers.
They're tearing up dear Mount Street.
It's got a torn-up face like Mick Jagger's.

I mean, this is Mount Street!
Scott's restaurant, the choicest oysters, brilliant fish;
Purdey, the great shotgun maker—the street is complete
Posh plush and (except for Marc Jacobs) so English.

Remember the old Mount Street,
The quiet that perfumed the air
Like a flowering tree and smelled sweet
As only money can smell, because after all this was Mayfair?

One used to stay at the Connaught
Till they closed it for a makeover.
One was distraught
To see the dark wood brightened and sleekness take over.

Designer grease
Will help guests slide right into the zone.
Prince Charles and his design police
Are tickled pink because it doesn't threaten the throne.

I exaggerate for effect—
But isn't it grand, the stink of the stank,
That no sooner had the redone hotel just about got itself perfect
Than the local council decided: new street, new sidewalk, relocate the
    taxi rank!

Turn away from your life—away from the noise!—
Leaving the Connaught and Carlos Place behind.
Hidden away behind those redbrick buildings across the street are
    serious joys:
Green grandeur on a small enough scale to soothe your mind,

And birdsong as liquid as life was before you were born.
Whenever I'm in London I stop by this delightful garden to hear
The breeze in the palatial trees blow its shepherd's horn.
I sit on a bench in Mount Street Gardens and London is nowhere near.

MOTO POETA

IN MEMORY OF STEPHEN A. AARON (1936–2012)

You were the loudest of us all by far,
And the sweetest behind your fear,
Brilliant expositor of Arthur Miller and Shakespeare.
There you are at the beginning of your career

Bellowing like a carny barker
In the Freshman Commons, selling tickets to some
HDC production with your tuba voice and bigger nose.
The stylish fellows like myself were appalled.

Steve Aaron was a lot brasher than was posh,
And a lot shyer, and smart.
Suddenly he was mounting a staging of Eliot's
Murder in the Cathedral to stop your head and start your heart,

The most gifted man in Harvard theater
In thirty years.
I remember him in Manhattan in analysis
Right across from the American

Museum of Natural History and its tattered old stuffed whale.
Aaron had an ungovernable phobic fear of the whale.
He asked me to go with him, literally holding hands,
So he could stare it down with an analytic harpoon—

And then backed out.
Years later, Goldie—his mother—pulled out of a closet
A brush and mirror set meant for a baby,
For baby Steve, and scrimshawed into the ivory back

Of each item was a tiny spouting whale!
The psychoanalyst's name was Tannenbaum.
One day Aaron came in and, after lying down, said: "I don't know why—
There's this tune I can't get out of my head! Tum *tum* tee tum. Tum *tum* te

O Christmas tree! O Christmas tree!" Steve,
You're a blue forest of oceans, seagulls flying their cries.
I come from an unimaginably different plan.
I've traveled to you because my technology can.

I ride the cosmos on my poetry Ducati, Big Bang engine, einsteinium fork
Let me tell you about the extraterrestrial Beijings and New Yorks.
You are dear planet Earth, where my light-beam spaceship will land.
I'll land, after light-years of hovering, and take your hand.

SCHOOL DAYS

I
John Updike

Updike is dead.
I remember his big nose at Harvard
When he was a kid.
Someone pointed him out on the street
As a pooh-bah at the Lampoon

As he disappeared into the Lampoon building
On Mt. Auburn.
The building should have seemed
Odd and amusing instead of intimidating,
But everything was intimidating,

Though one never let on.
Here was this strangely
Glamorous geek from New England,
With a spinnaker of a nose billowing out
From a skinny mast,

Only he was actually
Not from New England.
Those were the days when
One often didn't say hello even to a friend.
One just walked past.

I was a freshman in Wigglesworth
When I visited Ezra Pound
At St. Elizabeths,
And Updike was about to be *summa cum laude*
And go off to Oxford.

These were the days of Archibald MacLeish
And his writers' class in his office
In Widener for the elite.
I remember I put taps on my shoes
To walk out loud the long Widener reading room.

II
House Master

Mr. Finley sat cross-legged
On top of a desk
Reciting from memory Sappho in Greek
In his galoshes, administering an IV drip of nectar
While hovering like a hummingbird.

That was Finley, magical, a bit fruity,
Warbling like a bird while the snow outside
Silenced the Yard.
We were in a Romanesque redbrick
H. H. Richardson building, Sever Hall.

I was an auditor
In a Greek lyric poetry seminar
That was somewhere over the rainbow.
Certainly it was the only time
I heard a hummingbird sing.

I remember everything.
I remember nothing.
I remember ancient Greek sparkles like a diamond ring.
Professors were called mister.
To address someone as professor was deemed vulgar.

It was good sport to refer
To one's inferiors as N.O.C.D. (Not our class, dear.)
Biddies still cleaned the student rooms.
I had a living room with a fireplace that worked.
Finley was the master of Eliot House, my house.

Somewhere else, Senator Joseph McCarthy
Of Wisconsin was chasing American communists,
But despite that, he was evil.
The snow kept falling on the world,
Big white flakes like white gloves.

III
Pretending to Translate Sappho

The mother of the woman I currently
Like to spank, I'm not kidding,
Was my girlfriend at Harvard.
The mother looked like a goddess
And as a matter of fact majored at Radcliffe in Greek,

Or as we would say then,
That was her field of concentration.
Please don't tell me
Anyone reading this
Believes what I'm saying or doesn't, it's irrelevant.

But anyway it's all true.
I don't believe in biographies.
I don't believe in autobiography.
It's a sort of pornography
To display oneself swollen

Into bigger-than-life
Meat-eating flies.
I remember the mother on her bicycle
Flying across Harvard Yard
All legs.

Goddesses still wore skirts.
I'm still up to the same old tricks,
But now I'm always on time.
One time, I kept her waiting for me in the old
Hayes-Bickford Cafeteria on Mass. Ave. three hours.

When I finally got the goddess
Into my student bed,
The beauty of her nineteen-year-old body
Practically made me deaf, so loud
I leaked. My arrogant boy burst into tears.

IV
The Golden Bough

A tiger leaps on the back
Of a boy in the Yard for the kill.
The first warm day feels hot.
That's the Boston area's
Idea of spring, tearing winter violently

Apart a little before Reading Period,
In other words late,
So actually it's almost summer before it's spring.
Tropical parrots fly into the libraries and talk.
Two beautiful girls flaunt wide-brimmed summer hats.

Phyllis Ferguson is indescribable.
Elisabeth Niebuhr is the intellectual equivalent.
Both are in summer dresses
In honor of spring.
Each gets mentioned in *The Golden Bough*.

One girl went to Brearley.
One went to Chapin.
Those of you who know
What I'm talking about
Can stop reading.

The daughter of Reinhold Niebuhr rooms
With the granddaughter of Learned Hand,
Two knockouts—or rather four.
If you know what I'm talking about you nevertheless
Know it was spring

And blood was all over the Yard
Where the boy had been dragged and consumed.
Here comes the tiger with what looks like conjunctivitis
And, Jesus, he licks his lips
And looks exactly like what he ate.

V
Sweet Summer

I change a twenty for three tens
Could be the story of my life.
I give my bit and get a lot.
I give one back.
The sky is blue, the street fresh tar.

Tar smell. Smells like sweet summer.
Chi ci dà la luce? Il Duce!
That is to say, God.
Joe Lelyveld told me just now that Gandhi and Mussolini
Actually met. What an extraordinary thought.

Gandhi passing through Rome
On his way home.
Who knew Mussolini spoke English?
The language they used
To agree that Europe needed to change. Meaning no doubt

Their separate different things by that.
I hear the hiss of a hose.
I smell sunstroke kiss the cooling lawn.
The huge houses on Portland Place on their small lots
Are palazzi in Florence in old St. Louis.

Then came I to the shoreless shore of silence.
I stood there in Harvard Yard.
Huck Finn on his raft.
Harvard was all around me like the Mississippi
In the wet heat.

Heat shimmers upward from the hot.
Huck ties the fishing line to his toe so he can snooze
Alertly. It can make you crazy to be so happy
And on the verge of holy dictatorship and feeling you're a
Gandhi standing barefoot on a Mussolini balcony.

VI
Rejoice O Young Man in Thy Youth

Nelson Aldrich
Was so beautiful
He worried he was homosexual.
This was understandable.
So many men came on to him.

The Fay School, St. Paul's School, Harvard,
And his smile,
Are a certain kind of boy.
He joins the Porcellian.
He's not Everyman but he's American.

Every American boy worries
He's a fag, at least in those days
Did. I figure every boy at one
Stage or another is.
I never was,

Nor Nelson,
Even though he was called Nellie.
Not a nelly, but Nellie.
I call him Peter.
How rad is that!

BACK THEN

Negroes walking the white streets
Was how it seemed on Manhattan's Upper East Side.
One morning in 1971 it began.
I converted so to speak on the spot to the Ku Klux Klan.
My big blue heartfelt eyes hid in a hood and white sheets,
Completely ready to burn a cross and buy a gun.
A friend in the D.A.'s office said it's a gun or run.
I had thought these particular streets belonged to rich whites,
Almost as a matter of rich whites' civil rights.
The block on Seventieth between Park and Lexington Paul Mellon's sister
    sanctified.
The always Irish doormen along Fifth Avenue nearly died—
All of a sudden blacks were crossing over the border from their Harlem ho
And there were barbarians wandering the streets of Rome.
I knew the man who wrote this poem.

ANNUNCIATION

The simple water drinks from the drinking fountain in the waiting room,
And tastes happiness—tastes a sprig, a spring from the spout.
Fresh pours purely salt-free through
The sunshine pouring down on the glassy dunes
Of in vitro fertilization taking place in a clinic,
But you are also other things, O singing oasis, O oasis, O baby bird in a nest,
O innocence breast-feeding a rainbow,
Who change everything. New York is changed. Blessed art thou.

THE GREEN NECKLACE

I'm going out for a stroll and a bite and won't take myself with me.
Look after me while I'm gone, will you.
Outside the bleary windows is my sunny city.
I have to get the window cleaner in. Things change.
A day later, it's raining quite hard, and the dirt doesn't show.

We were both at some huge dinner party or other—this was her dream—
And you were sitting very far away from me.
I kept wondering whether
You would look over in my direction.
I kept trying not to look at you too much.

I have your green bead necklace on my desk.
I took it out of the drawer where I kept it after you left it.
Now I have it here, next to the computer.
I look down at it while I work.
I just touched it with my left hand.

How to survive a nuclear bomb.
I look out the binary window and see in—
The blinding flash and the blast and radiation—
See being dead talking to being alive, zero and one.
Look at me as a carton of cremains hailing a cab, or a man in love.

ARABIA

I move my body meat smell next to yours,
Your spice of Zanzibar. Mine rains, yours pours—
Sex tropics as a way to not be dead.
I don't know who we are except in bed.

I'll tell you someone I'm not happy with—
But no I won't. I won't destroy the myth.
The president of the United States
Is caught between those two tectonic plates,

Republicans and Democrats, the nude
Alternatives to naked solitude.
It's politics, it's tropics, and it's warm
Enough to arm the sunrise with a car alarm

That's going off and starts the earthquake shake
And shiver, shiver, of the sobbing steak.
O sweet tectonic fault line and sweet lips
Exuding honey that the cowboy sips.

I float in fluid to the other shore.
Ninth month. I scramble up the dune. I snore
Awake at sunrise with a snort. I turn
To touch the socket of the softest fern.

I got in line to vote and right away
I thought of you and years and yesterday
And how so much had changed and how it's true
Things do get better when you want them to.

My face between your thighs is resting there.
I'm happy staring at what makes me stare.
I see the psalm and it's a woman's labia,
My pornographically all-mine Arabia.

America keeps waiting to begin.
It's sunrise dripping from my chin.
It looks like spring out there on Broadway meant
Barack Obama to be president.

VICTORY PARADE

My girlfriend is a miracle.
She's so young but she's so beautiful.
So is her new bikini trim,
A waxed-to-neatness center strip of quim.

Now there's a word you haven't heard for a while.
It makes me smile.
It makes me think of James Joyce.
You hear his Oirish voice.

It's spring on Broadway, and in the center-strip mall
The trees are all
Excited to be beginning.
My girlfriend's amazing waxing keeps grinning.

It's enough to distract
From the other drastic act
Of display today—Osama bin Laden is dead!
One shot to the chest and one to the head,

SEAL Team 6 far away from my bed
Above Broadway—in Abbottabad, Pakistan, instead.
Bullets beyond compare
Flew over there,

Flew through the air
To above and below the beard of hair,
A type of ordnance that exploded
Inside the guy and instantly downloaded

The brains out the nose. Our Vietnam
Is now radical Islam.
I tip my hat and heart to the lovely tiny lampshade
Above her parade.

POEMS 1959–2009

I turn into the man they photograph.
I think I'll ask him for his autograph.
He's older than I am and more distinguished.
The beauty of the boy has been extinguished.
He smiles a lot and then not.
Hauteur is the new hot.
He tilts his nose up and looks imperious.
He wants to make sure he looks serious.
He smiles at the photographer but not
The camera. He thinks cold is the look that's hot.
You know the poems. It's an experience.
The way Shylock is a Shakespearience.
A Jew found frozen on the mountain at the howling summit,
Immortally preserved singing to the dying planet from it.

ARNAUT DANIEL

fictio rethorica musicaque poita
   —DANTE, *De vulgari eloquentia*

A shiver of lightning buckles the sidewalk.
Love cracks my sternum open
In order to operate,
Lays bare the heart, pours in sugar and chalk.
I open my mouth unable to talk.
I am someone having a bleed or a stroke.

I never stop talking,
Never lose consciousness,
Dying to be charming.
I stand there at liftoff
Burning lightning,
Basically blasting from the launch pad to kingdom come.

I am running in place on fire on a high wire,
Running into you in the shop,
And then outside
Can't stop. You have just come from a spin class—
O lovely smile miles away, that doesn't stop not
Coming closer.

Age is a factor.
A Caucasian male nine hundred years old
Is singing to an unattainable lady, fair beyond compare,
Far above his pay grade, in front of Barzini's on Broadway,
In Provençal, or it's called Occitan, pronounced *oksitan*, or it's that
I am someone else, whoever else I am.

Ezra Pound channeling the great troubadour poet Arnaut Daniel
In St. Elizabeths Hospital for the criminally insane
In Washington, D.C.,
Thanksgiving weekend, 1953,
I remember sounded like he
Was warbling words of birdsong.

THE STATE OF NEW YORK

I like the part I play.
They've cast me as Pompeii
The day before the day.
It's my brilliant performance as a luxury man because I act that way.
They say: Just wait, you'll see, you'll pay,
Pompeii.

You're a miracle in a whirlpool
In your blind date's vagina
At your age. Nothin could be fina.
You eat off her bone china.
Don't be a ghoul. Don't be a fool,
You fool.

In the lifelong month of May,
Racing joyously on his moto poeta to the grave,
He's his own fabulous slave.
He rides his superbike faster and faster to save
His master from the coming lava from China, every day,
But especially today, because it's on its way.

Fred Astaire is about to explode
In his buff-colored kidskin gloves, revolving around
The gold knob of his walking stick, with the sound
Of Vesuvia playing,
And the slopes of Vesuvia saying
Her effluvia are in nearly overflowing mode.

Freud had predicted Fred.
In *The Future of an Illusion* he said:
"Movies are, in other words, the future of God."
Nothing expresses ordinary wishes more dysplastically than current
American politics do. Breast augmentation as a deterrent
To too much government is odd.

Korean women in a shop on Madison give a pedicure to Pompeii.
Fred only knows that he's not getting old.
Pompeii doesn't know it's the day before the day.
The governor of New York is legally blind, a metaphor for his state of mind.
He ought to resign, but he hasn't resigned.
Good riddance, goodbye. The bell has tolled.

THE TERRIBLE EARTHQUAKE
IN HAITI

I think the truth is I have to go to the dentist.
That's what that quaking and shaking was all about.
God makes and breaks cheap cement! He's a cheap Cementist.
Both black people and white people
Have white teeth and shout
When God breaks the church and topples the steeple
In a tropical black country where almost every building is white.
I have to go to my New York dentist—who's also a guitarist—Arnie Mars,
And show him my dingy teeth are not right.
We'll talk the usual liberal bs.
I'll sit in his chair under the stars without electric light.
At least the air is warm.
At least I've been buried alive and can come to no further harm.
I'll shout whitely without an anesthetic while they amputate my arm.

LA CIVILISATION FRANÇAISE

In walks François Ier—only female, only beautiful—
Swims into the crowded room, big head like a tadpole,
Enormous nose and grandeur, and enormous eyes that pull
You to the bottom to deconstruct your soul.

The literary mermaid swimming toward you is a pearl
Whose whipping tadpole tail can break your back.
You want to make a double-decker with this girl?
Medic! It might explode. It might attack.

It's always somewhat Paris underneath New York.
But never mind—down there, beneath the tail, there's no way in.
The marvelous wine cellar of reds badly needs your cork!
Actually, not at all. There's no entry slit in the sleek mermaid skin.

One of these two is already an Immortal,
But for now is also just a man, if even that.
King Cobra stands staring at Queen Mongoose, swaying, looking for the
      portal,
Ready to sink a poem into her mortal fat.

"Quel péril, ou plutôt quel chagrin vous en chasse?"
"Cet heureux temps n'est plus. Tout a changé de face,
Depuis que sur ces bords les dieux ont envoyé
La fille de Minos et de Pasiphaé."

La fille de Minos et de Pasiphaé
Declaims from center stage in alexandrines her rouged rage
Which doesn't make a sound because there's nothing she can say,
And so it's time to turn the page.

In the East Village, on a sweet late-summer night,
A goddess dressed in Dior parts the party crowd.
A mouse stands staring at the Muse, at the amazing sight
Of a completely lovely François Ier, with the band blasting really loud

AT THE KNICK

My lining is reversible. I turn the Seidel sackcloth inside out and there's
The city and the evening and the Knickerbocker Club,
On whose posh porch across from Central Park who really cares:
It's summer and it's evening and we're smoking fine cigars!
They're Cuban lovelies and we'll puff them to a stub.
We're made of smoke, we Martians, and there's life on Mars.
I'm looking down at you from where we are,
A bit above Fifth Avenue, and you are walking by.
I see you from a distant star.
I see you in the shadows at the bus stop start to cry.
A Latin-looking woman in the outfit of a maid
Runs across the street to hand you something you
Perhaps had left behind, and runs away, as if she were afraid.
I turn that woman inside out and smell a zoo.

A TOAST TO LORIN STEIN

The butler wheeled Mrs. Waldheim out of her private elevator
And into the 1914 dining room
And a table set with goblets and massive gold flatware. I was ten.
This was St. Louis
Before the sun set on all this.

I think of Aldrich's roommate Derrick Nicholas
And dinner at Derrick's grandparents' in New York
Who dwelled in a mansion on Madison
Which took up much of the block,
Ancient and magnificent Dr. and Mrs. Seth Milliken.

I was talking about the early aviator Louis Blériot
When all of a sudden Dr. Milliken—who hadn't spoken in years—
Gasped: *I ADORED the fellow!*
We were terrified.
His nurse rose from her chair next to his and started to cry.

And apparently he never spoke again.
Aldrich became Paris editor of *The Paris Review*.
I followed him and Blair Fuller in the job. Youth! *Paris des rêves!*
Fifty years later, Barack Obama rules.
Lady Gaga reigns.

Lorin Stein seizes the *Paris Review* reins.
The joy or whatever
Of being the new editor begins, as it happens, April Fool's Day.
You know what I'm going to say.
I lift my glass to my friend.

RAINY DAY KABOOM

I get young when I'm not looking.
Or it happens when I turn out the light.
Sometimes I hear Indians
When I need to be scalped
And need to be helped.

How did it happen?
It happened overnight.
How come you got young?
They put my body in a pot.
They cut my feet off so I would fit.

They put my face in a fishbowl
So everybody could see it.
It floated around,
Looking for food.
Looking for a smile.

Then I saw you.
I saw you opening a black umbrella.
I saw you checking yourself in a lobby mirror.
I saw the flames leap like a cheerleader.
Sis boom bah.

I take the microphone and read
My poem "My Poetry"
For the podcast, at your request.
I doff my yarmulke.
My scalp, actually.

Welcome to South Waziristan.
I'm the Taliban.
I wrote their poem "My Poetry."
I meant it as an IED.
O say can you see me driving over it up-armored?

I ask to see the desk where you work so I can see.
Already at your request I've
Recorded Al Qaeda's poem "Death"
And the Taliban's "My Poetry."
I'm a roadside bomb singin' in the rain.

LISBON

Quite frankly, *nothing much happens.*
You walk downhill all day
From the fascistically monumental Four Seasons Hotel Ritz.
I have to say,
I've had a pleasant stay.
My Junior Suite makes me feel like Mussolini, it is huge.
I think of the edifice as Salazar in stone.
Salazar's slogan for Portugal was "Proudly alone,"
My kind of dictator.
He wanted a grand hotel in Lisbon
And arranged to have one.
I consider that admirable.
It's all downhill
From the hotel.
You walk downhill all day
On the Avenida de la Libertad and never lose your way.
You end up at the harbor. Obrigado.

And it's off in a cab to Brasileira, the café in Chiado
Where Fernando Pessoa spent so much time writing his immortal
Multiple-personality-disorder poems,
Now called Dissociated Identity Disorder.
That's where you find the statue.
That's where you pay homage.
He sits at a little bronze table outdoors

At the edge of the busy café tables, having an espresso
Made of bronze.
There is a chair next to his as part of the statue
So you can be photographed sitting next to him by someone.
I weep when we meet.
We bow deeply to each other.
His eyes mist over.
It is fate.
Tomorrow is Election Day 2008.
I'll fly nonstop Lisboa to Obama.

Really, the worst were the Portuguese.
But does it really make sense to talk about better and worse? Please!
In sixteenth-century Portugal, there were thirty-two thousand African slaves.
They came overseas in waves.
They sailed over in their graves.
It comes over me in waves.
They died and went on living. At Cabo de São Vicente, the black Atlantic
Spanks the gruesome cliff at the outer edge of Europe and gets sick,
Throwing up white.
The white is made of night.
The wrath fucks froth against the cliff.
Waterboarding makes the cliff stiff.
I voted for Obama and I ask Obama if.
Yes we can. I ask Pessoa.
I ask Lisboa. Did they know about the Shoah?
Yes we can.
We can do anything known to man.

It's heaven up there above the sky.
It's heaven down here, too.
I got to heaven without having to die.
It was a near-death experience with Bush 43. Phew.
But meanwhile the economy. So what are we going to do?
We're going to get through.
It's heaven up there above the sky.
Hey, it's heaven down here, too.
I love the future I won't live to see. I don't know why.
And don't even know if it's true.
Maybe I've already lived to see the future.
My multiple personalities climb to altitude on a single pair of wings.
Luxury Man rises to the top and Evening Man brings
To the podium the first African-American president to sing fado,
Chicago fado dado didi dado. Obrigado.
Please fasten your seat belts for takeoff, we're beginning our descent.
That isn't what I meant.

That long-ago Inauguration Day,
In a bitter cold Washington, D.C.,
The slender prince spoke without a hat or coat, elegance, eloquence.
His death in Dallas practically the next day was intense.
That's how the poem began.
It's time to leave the poem behind.
People saw a god trying to be a man.
People want to be blinded, to be blind.
The tragedy of Kennedy
Decanted me.
Beautiful things that go fast have enchanted me,
But it's time to leave Jack Kennedy and my motorcycles behind.

It is time to attend a new Inauguration.
It's checkout time at the Ritz in Lisbon.
The bill will be considerable.
I drank tons of their best port in my Baby Mussolini Suite.
I'm inside a seat belt on a plane. It's time to vote for victory over defeat.

Sieg Heil!
I said that to make you smile.
But you're not smiling.
(Why aren't you smiling?)
I said that to put you to sleep,
But you're Sieg Heiling.
I want to put you to sleep.
I think I'm falling asleep and I have a dream.
And everyone, come on everyone,
Come gather at the Lincoln Memorial!
Come together now! All together now!
And there is a woman singing.
I've fallen asleep in front of the set
And the vote keeps coming in
And millions of people are on the Mall.
And it is bitter cold.
And hopes are soaring! In the bitter cold they're ecstatically ignoring!

I face a yawning lion shaving in my mirror in the morning, roaring,
And there's my grandchild standing in the doorway, adoring—
Many teeth to brush, a beard to shave!
OK, it's not solace, but it's not nothing, still to be able to roar, to rave
With vim and vigor about the loss of vim and vigor.
It's sort of like a finger on a trigger

Is facing me in the morning mirror, and starts to snigger.
It's sort of like walking downhill in Lisbon
On the Avenida de la Libertad all day, but then I start to run
To get to the economy and Obama and the election—
Though I'd have to say,
I had a pleasant stay.
The breadlines in America will eventually go away,
And we will live to see another day.
A great leader lasts longer than a day.
The rain comes. The sun shines. He does not melt away.
A black man on a white horse shall chase the redskins away.

It's the dignity at Appomattox of Robert E. Lee
Live from Phoenix on TV.
That old white warrior John McCain gracefully concedes.
Nobly gives the nation what it needs.
A thousand years from now, you know it,
This day will be remembered, poet.
By the shores of Gitche Gumee,
By the shining Big-Sea-Water,
Told his message to the people,
Told the purport of his mission.
Car horns are celebrating up and down Broadway.
Tractor-trailer air horns joyously blasting.
Harlem to Times Square—Tribeca to Mecca.
Fado dado didi dado.
A nation conceived in liberty conceives.
Kids high-fiving, others crying.
Fado dado didi dado.

THEN ALL THE EMPTY
SHALL BE FULL

I see you in the morning and I see you in the evening.
That doesn't stop the other things.
The shorebirds and the shellfish make merry in the giant oil spill.
The fire drill bell rings and rings and rings.
Not everyone who wants to will.
I see you in the morning and I see you in the evening.

It's back to school. And, in our district, it is time to vote.
It's time to recognize it's fall,
And every larder will be full.
The fuel is mystical and has to be to feed us all.
I grab the supertanker by a hawser and I pull,
And rewrite everything I ever wrote.

THEY SHOW YOU THE HARP

Indeed, the human papillomavirus
Would seem to require us
To abjure oral relations,
Nutritious sixty-nine, the yodeling muff-divings and fellations.
Unless you want to be a dancer
With oral cancer,
There's your answer.
Stick to intercourse,
Though it's not safe either, of course.
Ride a horse.

The virus is spread
By love bugs in the bed.
And there is an unfunny increase in cancer of the mouth
Among the young, whose mouths are going south.
It's love. There's nothing else to talk about.
You end up with half your mouth cut out.
They used the Internet to elect their candidate
And lived on love and the little sleep they could get.
When you take a tour of a seniors' retirement home and they remove the
You see how deformed their hands are, and they show you the harp.

ISTANBUL

Stray dogs with a red plastic tag in one ear
Have been licensed
By the city to be safe and allowed to live in the street,
So they wander around, or more likely just lie there,
Healthy, checked by a city vet, without a care.
They're red-tagged Turks and they're an elite.
You walk past them in the street.
They're bums, they're the homeless, not educated.
It's complicated, but they're regulated.
It isn't complicated.
The red tag is their fez.
That's what the republic Atatürk founded says.

The Four Seasons Hotel Istanbul
Has toothsomely been called the best hotel in the world.
The luxury takes place in what was once a prison.
To be a prisoner of luxury
In the old center of the city
Is such a Turkish incarceration
To luxuriate in.
The Turkish hot chocolate the Four Seasons serves perspires
Oriental desires.
Think swarthy sweetness.
Think secular Atatürk.
But Sultanahmet has turned more than a bit Islamic.

From Claridge's and London I have come
To the holy city of Byzantium
To see Ayasofya.
I see the Blue Mosque and I see a
Fanta-zi-a projected on the air
Whose six minarets make it Disney beyond compare,
A fat, domed flying saucer with sticking-up spikes of hair.
I am awakened to the opposite of despair
By the Blue Mosque's muezzin's dawn call to prayer.
Another nearby mosque's muezzin immediately starts to call.
Come one, come all!
Antiphonally back and forth, and I go back to sleep.

I dream I'm dead in the trunk of a car. I'm the survivor.
I've hired for the morning a car and driver.
It's my Disney *Fantasia*
To drive to Asia.
Let's cross the Bosphorus.
It won't be hard for us.
Each day I take my pills from the day's section of the tray
Lest the Lord disappear me and throw me away.
I find myself across the bridge in Asia thinking of Aldo Moro.
Who on the Golden Horn thinks of Aldo Moro anymore, though?
I'm back at the Four Seasons.
The Red Brigades had their reasons.

Be so kind as to cover yourself please with the blanket, *presidente*.
We're going to drive you to another location for your safety.
So he covered himself.
Moretti immediately pumped
Eleven rounds into the blanket point-blank.
The car was left on a street pointedly
Equidistant from the Christian Democratic headquarters
And the Communist Party headquarters.
I'll stay in bed under the red bedspread.
A Turkish flag of red soaks the bed.
I'm better red and dead.
I'm full of bull in Istanbul.

Awake!
Listen to the Voice! Climb out of the trunk! Rise and shine!
The bullet-riddled Moro is divine.
Each bullet hole is a portal to the immortal.
I've breathed so many million tears my legs ache.
My fellow Armenians, my brain is about to break.
I walk up the hill to Topkapi Palace past the red-tagged dogs.
I've heisted so much bullion.
I've lived a life of luxury.
I've lived my own Topkapi of poetry.
I've lived through four seasons. The muezzin calls.
The dueling muezzins call. It's dawn. It's dark. I SEE.

TRANSPORT

The time is coming when it won't be maintenance.
The time is coming when it won't be minimal.
I walk with my long-dead dog up a hill.
We're walking in the Cher in France.
I'm worried about the coming presidential election.
I realize I'm dreaming but it's real.
I'm in my bed but what I feel
Is happiness that goes beyond Manhattan.
I'm sprinting up the familiar steps to cast my vote.
Two minutes later I've already forgotten
The pink rose made of meat inside my skull is rotten—
And I'm floating off the bed. I start to float.

Everywhere in French Polynesia I flew Air France.
Each island hop I told the stewardess or pilot
I was learning to fly and would love to visit the cockpit.
Here I am floating off a runway in a cockpit trance
In a jumbo jet
Going back to Paris. Goodbye, Papeete—
Many years ago, and many wars—and maybe
It's coming but it's not here yet.
Tons of weight ooze into the sky without a cough,
With me practically at the controls in the cramped third seat.
Even back then, pre-9/11, only a Frenchman could invite
A student pilot into the cockpit of a brand-new jumbo jet for takeoff.

I'm on an elephant and I am higher than you.
I am enormously proud and my trunk can pull up a tree.
I am as big as a jumbo jet about to crash into the sea.
A terrorist on board has blown it apart—the plane has split in two.
People are spilling out of the windows of the buildings,
Or are jumping out to escape the vaporizing heat
And exploding when they hit the street.
I know I put them somewhere—I am looking for my water wings—
So I can float above the island of Sifnos,
And float over Disney Hall in downtown Los Angeles,
And float over Ryōan-ji and the Kyle of Lochalsh.
Bring back the *Hindenburg* please God to transport all of us.

OEDIPAL STRIVINGS

A dinosaur egg opens in a lab
And out steps my paternal grandfather, Sam,
Already taller than a man,
And on his way to becoming a stomping mile-high predator, so I ran.
I never knew my mother's father, who may have been a suicide.
He was buried in a pauper's grave my mother tried
To find, without success. Jews grab
The thing they love unless it's ham,
And hold it tightly to them lest it die—
Or like my mother try
To find the ham they couldn't hold.
A hot ham does get cold.
Grampa, monster of malevolence,
I'm told was actually a rare old-fashioned gentleman of courtly benevolence.

At night the thing to do was drive to Pevely Dairy
And park and watch the fountain shooting up and changing colors.
The child sat in the back, finishing his ice-cream soda,
Sucking the straw in the empty glass as a noisy coda.
Sometimes on Sunday they drove to the Green Parrot.
There was the sideways-staring parrot to stare at.
The chickens running around were delicious fried, but nothing was sanitary.
B.O. was the scourge of the age—and polio—and bathroom odors.
If you didn't wash your hands,

It contributed—as did your glands!
His father always had gas for their cars from his royal rationing cards.
The little boy went to see the king at one of the king's coal yards.
The two of them took a trip and toured the dad's wartime coal mine.
It was fun. It was fine.

The smell of rain about to fall,
A sudden coolness in the air,
Sweetness wider than the Mississippi at its muddy brownest.
I didn't steal his crayon, Mrs. Marshall, honest!
It's CAPTAIN MIDNIGHT . . . brought to you by OVALTINE!
I travel backwards in a time machine
And step inside a boy who's three feet tall.
How dare he have such curly hair!
A boy and his dog go rafting down the Mississippi River.
They have a message to deliver
To the gold-toothed king.
Sire, we have a message that we bring.
Little boy, approach the throne.
Ow! I hit my funny bone.

The British consul was paid extra because it was a hardship post.
The weather was Antarctica/equatorial extreme.
Surely summer was in error.
Winter was terror.
White snowflakes the size of dinosaur eggs
Versus humidity that walked across your face on housefly legs.
I loved both the most.
Radio made women dream

Of freedom from oppression and the daily nonsense.
Hairy tarantulas in boatloads of bananas made the lazy heat immense
In the heart. Blizzards didn't stop my father's big blue coal trucks so why
    bother.
Why bother, father?
Billie Holiday was inside.
I thought I had gone to heaven and died.

NEWS FROM THE MUSE

This is what it's like at the end of the day.
At the end of the day, homosexuals are gay.
Pundits love to say, "at the end of the day."
"Bottom line" is their other cliché.
The end of the day will go away,
But we heterosexuals are here to stay.
Sunlight preoccupies the cross street.
It and night soon will meet.
Meanwhile, there is Central Park.
Now the park is getting dark.

I said to my own personal, private Central Park last week,
I said to her: Look at me, just take a little peek.
I said it's the difference between day and night,
That's what's exciting, because it's so right.
I'm remembering with amusement how she treated me
At the state dinner, how she greeted me
With incredible coldness, which was a trick,
Since she was so excited she was almost sick,
So excited she let loose a lake
And rowboats you can rent for a trip you can take.

I'll walk around the Reservoir with you
And then walk down Fifth Avenue
To the Met to the show just opened of Samurai arms and armor.
I'm an armored charmer.
I'm room after room of gleaming display
Of blade after blade and by the way
This is what it's like at the end of the day
When the sword of art has its say.
Fifth at Eighty-second
On the edge of the park has beckoned.

The American Museum of Natural History, on Central Park West,
On the other side of the park from the art, offers its breast.
Art after all is lies.
Art is tadpoles that think they have a right to grow up to be butterflies
And croak and flutter among flowers.
Seriously, why not do away with set museum hours
And let the killers come and go among the exhibits at dawn if they want,
Without adult supervision? Dripping blood, they'll hunt
The mounted specimens in the wildlife dioramas,
But grow up to be sweetly smiling Dalai Lamas.

I'm the Art of the Samurai. I have nothing to fear.
I have a sword and the way is clear.
I have the weapon to love anyone who comes near.
I always walk back across the park from the Met at this time of year.
I walk back and forth in my study till I hear
The words pour into the computer like sunlight, in my ear.
The computer splits a brick with one chop of my hand and sheds a tear

For the brick, but, my dear,
They are crocodile tears, and completely insincere.
The poem you're reading now will eventually appear.

A filthy city pigeon has landed on my desk to say
It will wait for me on the ledge outside the window while I pray.
It's got to be the Annunciating Angel from the way it moans and coos
That it expects the poem that's coming to bring good news.
Now we're flying above Central Park,
And there I am down there looking up at me and shouting, *Hark!*
I flirt across Sheep Meadow and the Great Lawn,
A little brief thing shyer than a fawn,
But shouting with everything it has, *It's true!*
At the end of the day, it's you.

SWEET DAY, SO COOL, SO CALM, SO BRIGHT

Give me Gandhi telling the poet Tagore, in a feisty mood:
"The hungry millions ask for one poem—invigorating food."
I'm crossing a desert looking for a dessert.
I lick the dirt.
I am hungry and unhappy and look and see
It looking at me
From under her skirt.
I see a delightful little hair shirt.
I see a valley of moist Montale plus myself plus George Herbert.
Wait here. Stay alert.

When the red apples are ready on the trees,
Don't you feel like saying, "Apples, please,
Instead of providing cider,
You could be a better provider
If you gave us summer back."
I would instantly trade apple flesh and crunch for a black
Atlantic of yellow waves under a warm moon in August.
Give me back the Harley-Davidson hog of lust
I rode when I was July and rutting,
When I was in rut, instead of being in a rut putt-putting.

The Sunday-morning TV talk shows by Sunday noon are yesterday.
They had their say. They've gone away.
Now it's noon.
I'm standing on a dune

Listening to the sound the waves make,
Which is the hiss of a bandage being pulled off, *Ow, for Christ's sake!*
Only it feels *good*, the extreme opposite of hurt.
Waves and gulls will always flirt.
Reaches up under her skirt.
Ow! rips off his shirt.

O black-and-yellow moonlit sea,
O fattest black-and-yellow August bumblebee,
I struggle to shut my snout.
I burst out in the street like someone just let out.
The big movie screen in the sky
Is covered with stars, who wave *Hi*.
It's Iran, or it's Afghanistan
And the Taliban.
Bad apples fall and rot,
Or not.

Stay with me a few more minutes and give me Gandhi.
Give me the great Bolognese painter Morandi.
Give me stout-hearted men of their severe purity,
Saints who don't have sex who constitute a threat to Homeland Security.
Her posterior is superior. I thank it. I spank it.
Her hair down there is my bib, my crib, my security blanket.
When there's this much chiming rhyming, check around you, look behind y
Behind you—and it defined you—
You sat in the corner eating hair pie,
And you lifted your head and said, What a good boy am I.

CUNNILINGUS

The recently reopened Great Lawn seemed
Too green to use and was.
They roped it off again.
It was too young.

The grass was greener on the other side.
Not ready to be eight baseball fields.
I wanted to get down on my hands and knees and eat grass
Like a beast.

Not ready to have the pope
Pray in front of five hundred thousand.
Out of respect
For Her Holiness, I took my shoes off.

You were my outlook and my prosody.
You were the call to prayer five times a day.
You were the be-all and end-all of a forehead pressed to the floor.
You made me take my shoes off to protect your new floors.

Five hundred thousand tuchuses
With faces, with tongues out
To receive communion, were your humble servant me
Swaying in your palm-tree breeze.

You were my sound track.
You were my sound check.
I heard the muezzin summoning my forehead callus
To the mosque.

Obama is my president.
Too much is almost enough at the end of a life.
I am aware that my dark hair could be dyed.
My face is falling off my face.

POINTER IN THE FIELD

A hunting dog freezes in the pose
And points his muzzle at the bird.
The dog's heart has a hard-on.
The implied gun goes off.
The bird bursts into flames.
The bird bursts into song.
The woman flies away
To come again another day.

PALM SUNDAY

Manhattan shrinks to a tiny tooth
Of towers far below as we accelerate violently into verse and space
And leave the road behind.
Congress is having a stroke, and it's a heart attack, and it can't face
China and the truth
Fulminating from Duluth.
Everest is the penthouse of the Earth and God is on my mind,
But I'm more interested in getting off the Earth to your Down Under.
My spirituality is to go hypersonic—
And fly hypersonically out of New York on the Hampton Jitney to
    Sagaponack,
Where the grass is green as the green of a Memling and the sky is you,
Where the gulls cry with white wings and the waves gush fresh as dew.
The time has come for magnitudes of thunder
To split the vast nonsense of death asunder.

My subject is New York outside my window where
The world is a mirage in the nude.
My subject is the Sunday-morning TV talk shows, which I,
Loving politics, eat like food.
I must say, Palm Sunday means nothing to me. I don't care.
It's almost time to nail Christ to the air.
It's almost Easter and the pundit in the sky.
I hope there really is another universe—
New evidence says there must be—where Jesus isn't born,

Nor the Buddha, nor Muhammad, all that porn.
Evidence indeed suggests other universes, nursed by the universe breast,
The Big Bang being the breast, the first suck being the best,
Because that suck is the void in reverse.
Then came the Pharisees, Pontius Pilate, six million Jews killed, and worse.

Close your eyes while you read this
Default setting for the Divinity.
It's Muhammad in the cave and the angel commanding: *Recite!*
Close your eyes to see infinity.
God bless the bliss
Of the kiss
Of Judas Iscariot that won't come out right,
But comes out right. It's in 3-D. It's an illusion.
Mecca today in the Arab sunlight is a white bridal gown.
The Buddha smiling at a stoplight sees the red nose of a clown.
The Central Park Zoo barking seals that you love, darling,
Sun themselves in the same sunlight as the talkative starling
Who imitates a car alarm, saying thereby that the world is delusion
And the Holocaust merely a contusion.

Broadway is kneeling next to my building. Christ
Mounts the ass to go into town.
Gautama is teaching on Seventy-ninth at the corner.
Muhammad rides through Harlem in a white convertible with the top down.
God the stallion and God the gelding is sliced
Into bite-sized portions, they put out a contract on him, iced,
Into the river in cement shoes, ends up at the coroner
Astronomer who is looking for complicity,
For sympathetic understanding from a universe

Turning violently into verse.
A poem should not mean but be.
Oh really?
My poems have the cedar simplicity
Of a shoe tree.

Picture me in front of the TV
Staring at a mirage.
The events of the week in the world break the flat-screen surface like fish.
They are caught and cleaned and cooked and given a massage.
I'm climbing the dunes of the Sahara with a mermaid swimming toward n
Talking away, as if she were afraid she'd already bored me.
I hear her emphatic politics, spoken in English English,
Part of the TV panel of pundits in Washington, D.C., on this Palm Sunday.
When I escape to the window for a moment to breathe New York,
Something white is flying through the sky that is not a stork.
I think about people who have died and are dead.
I don't think they have gone somewhere else instead.
I don't think I will see them again one day.
I don't think China will overtake the U.S. before Monday.

THEY'RE THERE

IN MEMORY OF FRANK KERMODE (1919–2010)

At least the dead don't have to die.
Everyone you see is dead, but it's the Hamptons, so get over it.
Edward, and next Dick—and now Frank—all dead. Boys, goodbye.
Frank, at ninety, said on the phone he didn't particularly want to die.
Don't try to tell Frank that his charming work won't die.
The dead don't give a shit
About their work once they die. Frank is the newcomer:
I look around the lawn and there is everyone.
Poirier and Said and Kermode are sipping white wine and it is summer.
The fancy world of dead is having fun.
Everyone is wearing summer light.
They can't tell wrong from right.

ONE LAST KICK FOR DICK

IN MEMORY OF RICHARD POIRIER (1925–2009)

Old age is not for sissies but death is just disgusting.
It's a dog covering a bitch, looking so serious, looking ridiculous, thrusting.
The EMS team forces a tube down your airway where blood is crusting.
Imagine internal organs full of gravel oozing and rusting.
An ancient vase crossing the street on a walker, trudgingly trusting
The red light won't turn green, falls right at the cut in the curb, bursting, busti
You're your ass covered with dust that your dust mop was sick of dusting.
The windshield wipers can't keep up. The wind is gusting.
A massive hemorrhagic bleed in the brain stem is Emerson readjusting.

Why did the fucker keep falling?
I'm calling you. Why don't you hear me calling?
Why did his faculties keep failing?
I'm doing my usual shtick with him and ranting and railing.
You finally knocked yourself unconscious and into the next world
Where Ralph Waldo Emerson, in the ballroom of the mind, whirled and twirl
Fifty-three years ago, at the Ritz in Boston, we tried one tutorial session in the
You got so angry you kicked me under the table. Our martinis turned black as
And all because your tutee told you Shakespeare was overrated. I went too far

WHAT NEXT

So the sun is shining blindingly but I can sort of see.
It's like looking at Mandela's moral beauty.
The dying leaves are sizzling on the trees
In a shirtsleeves summer breeze.

But daylight saving is over.
And gaveling the courtroom to order with a four-leaf clover
Is over. And it's altogether November.
And the Pellegrino bubbles rise to the surface and dismember.

RAIN

Rain falls on the Western world,
The coldest spring in living memory everywhere.
Winter in mid-May means the darling buds of May uncurled
On an ice-cold morgue slab, smilingly shaking loose their beautiful hair.
London rains every day anyway.
Paris is freezing. It's May, but Rome is cold.
Motorcycles being tested at the factory in Varese north of Milan are gray
Victims screaming in place and can't get out and won't get sold.

It's the recession.
It's very weird in New York.
Teen vampires are the teen obsession,
Rosebud mouths who don't use a knife and fork.
Germany at first won't save Greece, but really has to.
It's hot hot in parts of Texas, but rain drowns Tennessee, people die.
It's the euro. It's the Greek debt. Greece knew
It had to stop lying, but *timeo Danaos*, they're Greeks, Greeks lie.

Canoeing in the Ozarks with Pierre Leval: the rain came down so hard
The river rose twenty-three feet in the predawn hours and roared.
Came the dawn, there was improbably a lifeguard,
There was a three-legged dog, the jobless numbers soared.
Dreamers woke in the dark and drowned, with time to think this can't be tr
Incomprehensible is something these things do.
They bring the Dow Jones into the Ozarks and the Ozarks into the EU.
A raving flash flood vomits out of a raindrop. The Western world is in the l

Entire trees rocket past. One wouldn't stand a chance in the canoe.
A three-legged dog appears, then the guy it belongs to.
You instantly knew
You'd run into a hillbilly backwoods crazy, itching to kill you.
Berlin and Athens, as the Western world flickers,
Look up blinking in the rain and lick the rain and shiver and freeze.
They open black umbrellas and put on yellow slickers
And weep sugar like honeybees dying of the bee disease.

EGYPT ANGEL

I'm not on your side, whichever side you're on.
My enthusiasm for Nasser is long gone.
Hail, Hosni Mubarak, and farewell!
There's the old dictator dolt
On TV, a contraption of dyed hair and hair gel.
Angels in revolt
Fill Tahrir Square. The angel Gabriel blows his horn
To announce to the reborn: *You've been born!*
And Koranically commands: *Recite!*
Here are the things that are right!
Day after day of secular celebration turns into night.
Not too many people are killed.
People are thrilled.

I'm your fat King Farouk,
Quacking poetry till I puke.
I'm president and premier and sultan and emir—
Prime minister and Sadat—
And oh my God he's been shot!
I do nothing but think about you, dear.
I think about you a lot.
I revere
The crypto-philo-Semite Anwar Sadat,
And what he did, and in consequence the death he got.
The third president of Egypt agreed to put up with Israel.
He slithered through the Arabs like an eel.
It did not go down well.

The West oinked for oil and said please.
The Western nations hung out backstage like groupies.
They barked to be fed, like a seal.
They stole anything they could steal.
Anwar Sadat screwed the lightbulb of love into the socket
Out loud in the dark in the middle of the night.
Floaters swim by in my eye in the light.
Darling, don't doubt me, don't knock it.
I fold a linen handkerchief to make three points
To fountain whitely toward you from my breast pocket.
Point 1. My cornea detaches.
Point 2. I have galloping myopia.
Point 3. My cataracts won't let me look at you.

It's lenticular astigmatism.
It's macular degeneration.
A rainbow coalition of coition ejaculates
A colorblind wine jelly of jism
And every radical ism.
White Europeans conceived these wretched Arab states,
Now fictively becoming democrats.
The breeze blows the blue of the sea
Inland from Tripoli.
Meet me in Tahrir Square.
Righty-o, I'll meet you there.
Your Nile-green eyes gaze up at me from the pillow.
Baby, you're my crocodile Nile. You're my Cairo.

Tahrir Square is twirling like a dervish, spinning like a top.
In Tahrir Square tear-gas canisters pop.
My crocodile angel joins the demonstrators outside her shop.
The tornado funnels into focus from a censored blur.
The military clears a path for her.
Democracy is in the vicinity
Of Nefertiti.
We'll meet in Tahrir Square.
Every angel has gathered there,
Including my own angel, wings of Isis flapping.
Bandages are unwrapping
The royal mummy, who's been napping, but opens her charms.
My Egypt angel wraps me in her arms.

TRACK BIKE

The bicycle messenger who nearly knocked you over
Was me trying to.
That was me circling Columbus Circle
On a track bike, the kind with one gear and no brakes.
Look out! No brakes with a message!
I flashed around the velodrome
Of my life, clinging to your steeply banked curves,
And discovered the New World.

It's as if your body were itself a person
And the person wasn't you.
It's as if I were a flesh-eating flower,
Whereas actually I'm originally from St. Louis.
The performing self opens the stage door.
I start my act.
I feel like running for office.
I feel like riding a fixed-wheel track bike for the simplicity.

You'll play the viola
And I'll play myself.
Komm, süsser Tod
Comes out of my mouth
Like a tail coming out of a dog.
Take my hand and we'll wag down Fifth Avenue.
We'll walk into the first church we see,
Which is to say the Apple Store.

I'm walking west on Central Park South
With my iPhone out.
I am calling you, oo oo oo, oo oo oo,
With a love that's true, oo oo oo, oo oo oo.
We take the Time Warner Building
Escalators up the four floors to the top.
Something about how incredible it all is
Tells me to stand back from the edge of the vertiginous view.

I get dizzy imagining I'm on the balcony
That runs around the torch of the Statue of Liberty
Looking down on Columbus Circle.
The handlebars are in my hands.
I ride without brakes around and around.
I walk around the torch blazing.
I see you thirty blocks uptown
In my bed, light pouring in.

And we have tickets for the Bach at Lincoln Center.
And let's check out
The Upper West Side Apple Store next door.
It's one more crystal-clear Apple cathedral
For Saint Steve Jobs, who discovered America,
Where the deer and the antelope play
With the herds of touch screens on display,
Not far from Columbus Circle and pancreatic cancer.

9 780374 534059